I0475734

The 10 Commandments of Enterprise
The Rules of Reigning in Your Niche'

The 10 Commandments of Enterprise

The Rules of Reigning in Your Niche'
by
DC JAMES

Copyright © 2013 by DC JAMES
All rights reserved. No part of this book may be reproduced, scanned, or
distributed in any printed or electronic form without permission.
Published By Red Wrighter Books
First Edition: February 2013
Printed in the United States of America
ISBN: 978-1-300-78631-3

EXCLUSION

Leave the egos right here before you read on ...

This is the part of us that toggles between our conscience and subconscious sense of reality, or at least trying to make sense of reality. I make this request for the benefit of transformational learning taking place. Especially to you who are of brilliant mind; resolute in your convictions toward what is worthy of your time and endorsement.

PLEASE turn off your smart devices ...

Dropping your guard is appropriate in a setting where there's no cause to be alarmed. There's no agenda to intrude or invade the practices of your personal or business acumen. Note: Becoming viral involves being vulnerable. You say it sounds irresponsible. It appears counter-intuitive. That's the self-absorbed filter talking now.

Turn that off also...

If you are taking on the challenge of developing a personal competitive edge or creating a top notch team; you're going to need the right commands for a commanding presence in your niche' or best business practice.

Lets turn this on and up ...

These commands are directives. They are value based. They are imperatives entrusted to those who have authority, aspire to greatness and a sense of destiny. The only threat is suffering the consequences of misappropriating and abusing them to forcibly control your enterprise and or neglecting to implement them. They are true. They are tested. They are tender.

Lets turn things around ...

Table of Contents

THE COMMANDMENT OF APPRECIATION

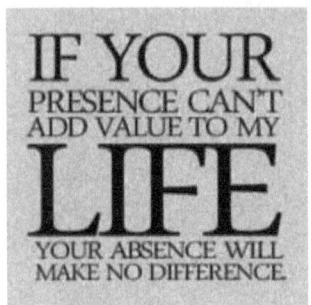

Your Beliefs are Value Systems. More specifically your e-value-ation process *is* your value system. Things become valuable because of evaluation. This commandment establishes belief in oneself and in others. We attach a note of trust to things proven to be reliable, dependable and consistent in fulfilling expectations. In fact, we esteem the little things very highly. Worth is estimated by appraisal. And those same appraisals are given through a comparison analysis of one thing against the other – or one business against another and so on.

There are many things that are costly but add no value. Conversely, there are things of great value that don't cost a fortune. And some things *are* priceless. This doesn't mean "cheap", but it does mean money can't buy, compare or match its worth.

"Value Is Measured By the Worth We Give Others"

One way for an enterprise to Add Value is through Endorsement.

QUESTIONS?
- When people are in your presence do you increase or decrease their WORTH?
- Regardless of your genius, wealth or status, do you give others CONFIDENCE?
- Do you bring them in touch with their GREATNESS?

INSIGHT: Belief =*Living on a Being.*

Language that says, *"I want to be like ..., "I wish I could do like ...* pay attention too. Adding value of praise and appreciation is a reflection of how you and or your enterprise behave in your roles and responsibilities. It's the "attitude heath" imparted into and impressed upon others from a direct connection of who we are "being". The opposite is true with harsh and depreciative language –evil communication corrupts good mannerisms. The affects of your organization, membership, or practice trace back to belief or disbelief. An enterprise's "buy in" toward its own results is the life spark that convinces others to buy.

APPLICATION:
If you love something, it ought to look like something.

This is how others come to respect what you respect. You establish a value system for them by your own behavior towards something. This is in connection with who you emulate. People follow others not by what others know or think, but when they see that there's care. Some who are grossly lacking esteem are better suited with an imputing challenge to gain virtue rather than misappropriating or mixing words to patronize which only panders to the ego. In other words, don't talk down to your staff or your customers not even to yourself. Speak highly at all times. It is a "reflection" that cast back a positive image of how you evaluate things. This is where it pays to be in good company and in close association with those who make good impressions.

THE COMMANDMENT OF AUTHORIZATION

Empowerment is the Working Capital of Authority. Much is abused when power is involved but that's where regulation will channel such forces. I speculate that many of us confuse "deregulation of authority" as *Entitlement* to authority. Let's look at the possible causes. The obvious can be attributed to immaturity but another cause may stem from poor examples of leadership; abuse of power demonstrated by the high offices of government, business and social culture. Our media outlets grossly exploit this. This frenzy for catching leaders in the "*cookie jar*" or with their "*pants down*" only serves to undermine the validity of authority. It gives license to peers and subordinates to go around the system and circumvent authority.

The remedy for the government, communities and business enterprises with a skewed view of empowerment is reform. This begins first with the mind. The best place to start in your organizational environment is around the structure of policy and the rules of conduct. Remember, power is intoxicating. It is not to be coveted or taken casually and especially not given to a novice. You can't possess power when it possesses you.

On the contrary, Empowerment is purposeful in executing authority. It is not for electrocuting with punitive intentions - regardless of just cause. Too often we condition others to FAIL by not "PER-MISSIONING" them with invested authority. This investment of power is most effective with a clear understanding of the terms, conditions and accountability that goes with it.

An example of having authority and no empowerment is like telling a soldier "GO TAKE THAT HILL!" but never giving him resources or special instruction. He takes the hill by using "any means necessary" only to return to the ranking officials to receive a barrage of epitaphs, demerits or criticism of why didn't he do it another way.

IF ONLY WE WE'RE MIND READERS

This sort of practice is not uncommon. Most will attest they were either the victim or the victimizer affected by the tentacles of this "demoralizing" monster created out of assumptions. And there's a chance it stems from misappropriated authority. Let's say in your case you were desperate giving authority to an ambitious novice or an overzealous veteran who's trying to make a name for himself in the twilight hours of his career. Let's face it, sometimes it's best to have an area of silence until the right candidate comes along, than having a place of chaos.

> *"Order doesn't come out of Chaos.*
> *Order enters into Chaos and makes it behave."*

BY POWER DIVESTED

Just as a battery starts a car, it would be a hazard to the other working parts if there wasn't a *"voltage regulator."* This regulator properly supplies the correct current levels throughout the electrical system. Much in the same way does our roles and responsibilities regulate within an enterprise. We should take *charge* with ability, self-control and humility of mind. Oftentimes we witness others take *over* with inability, loss of control and pride of mind.

This is the bolt of the hinge to understanding empowerment. That we are only conduits; parts that the current flows through. Those empowered are not the "Power." Not understanding this we disqualify ourselves; going from hopeful prospects to unusual suspects as it regards exercising authority (*remember* <u>Disney's Sorcerer's Apprentice</u>).

NOTE: Bear this in mind, there's a thin line between the Tyrant and the Templar; good initiative and bad judgment. It would be best to be summoned by the king rather than announcing your own arrival.

BY POWER INVESTED

Once the criteria of authority, delegated or deferred are determined by the enterprising culture all observing agents can ratify them. Once in place the standard becomes a measure that sorts out and sizes up all eligible candidates. The aim is to rule out bias, preference and prejudice. This allows the Standard, based on the values, mission and vision to back up the person who becomes empowered to carry out the duties of the enterprise with full backing and authority.

THE COMMANDMENT OF INVOLVEMENT

The Root Word of Ignorance is Ignore. In the information age that we live in, little is left hidden and undisclosed. We have access to things readily available, "literally" through a digital medium paved on an electron highway, on a global scale. The perceptive and informed would say, "There is no excuse to be in the dark". The reality is that there are dead spots in transmission and delays in translation. Not every surfer catches the "informational wave". And to most anything new is perceived as a "craze". Alas, Ignorance is bliss, but also "blistering" to the ill informed and the unlearned.

"Careware is the new Shareware"

DEFINITION OF AWARENESS:
The precautionary behavior and responsive insight through "informing" the intuition.

You have a duty to be aware and to make others aware of crucial information that has bearing on their functions and all other's collectively within your enterprise. No doubt we respond accordingly to the 911's of life's distresses but when it comes to the 411's (info), and the 611's (cust. service) our reflexes are stifled and numbed by suspicion, apathy, and illiteracy. These responses misinterpreted as admirable traits of precaution makes it worst.

No question, you should always be aware of things that would harm your business, i.e. public reporting of loss, trade secrets etc. But the greater value is gained from the proper emphasis and use of all information good or bad. As an enterprise it is crucial how you make use of the public's record about you, survey analysis and industry reports. Everything can work to your good, but that will depend on the way you manage awareness.

Some of us remember the Tylenol scare in the early 80's. And the Jack-n-the-Box franchise that encountered e coli poisonings in the late 90's or the turbulence of recent years with bad tomatoes, spinach and cantaloupes. These were costly lessons that affected all industries because of public trust. All these "outbreaks" are now outtakes brought under control. And was it resolved by suspicion, finger pointing or witch-hunts? Quite the contrary. They were mitigated by awareness, yes an acute involvement to translate the information to all who needed to know.

ONLY RESPONSIBLE FOR WHAT YOU ARE AWARE OF

Don't leave your post chasing the wind.
Whatever grabs your attention doesn't warrant your permission.
You may see movement but that doesn't require you to move.
There is "thrill" in the chase but acquire "thrift" in the choice.
The benefit to your enterprise during these times will be to employ patience and self-control and not be given to chase.
Employ involvement as a group-think-activity.

A RECIPE FOR INVOLVEMENT

Here is a little tongue twister exercise emphasizing involvement you can use as an ice breaker or a teaser: pooled-peaked-persons-perceptions-preemptively-planning-profitable-practices

Do not assume everyone who's involved knows what's going on. It is important not to withhold wisdom from the wanderer or disadvantage the simpleton by leaving them to themselves. Wisdom is community property with no copyright owners. Conversely, nor is it acceptable to tolerate the excuses of the willful, the illiterate, and the handicapped. Create zones and designated areas for dissemination, but do not accommodate the "least of these" *(in etiquette, decorum and scruples)* by paving a completely new road to access and acquire information.

Involvement requires every effort available to fulfill everything necessary for the moment. It doesn't need the brawn of our faculties to figure out how to get everyone on the same page. The softer side of awareness is in agreement, assurance and affirmation. These require no oaths and no vows.

PEOPLE HEAR BETTER THROUGH CIRCUMSTANCES

Although most of us are born with ears, we don't use them as much as we should. But I guarantee you, regardless of gender, nationality or language, we all hear through circumstances of danger better than hearing words in our own native tongues. From Sun Tzu's Art of War, he suggests the use of signals, sounds and banners as useful in communicating in adverse conditions or because of great distances. Frankly, sometimes silence can do the heavier lifting **(meaning**: *over explaining can cause more confusion)*. This is by showing no protest and a quite resolve. Suggestion: handle the duties of making your enterprise aware of things as one who has a "neighborhood watch" assignment. Your reasonable service, whatever the field, is being alert to alert those who need to know.

#4 *You Should Be Responsible*
THE COMMANDMENT OF RESOLUTION

Responsibility is the Ability to Respond. The new revolution is the revolution of responsibility. In your planning you must become resolute in reprimanding irresponsible activity that would jeopardize standards, values and quality. Reprimand what you require; actions of others as well as your own. The practice of resolution is making appropriate provisions to "adjust" situations in the way that they should go. Correction initially is unpleasant for most of us. It's a delayed appreciation after swallowing bitter pills.

"In All Things be More Careful and Less Sorry."

The responsibility for keeping short accounts on offense is greatly needed and seldom exercised. All too often in enterprises, disagreements can turn into fits that lead to feuds. Conflict resolution is an acquired skill. So is disciplining personal disappointments. It will take such skill to navigate through undesirable states of behavior. Whereas by default, we have become professionals at keeping record of every wrong perpetrated against ourselves and others. We become victims building our case instead of victors leading our cause. And that case being, "I'm hurt and somebody has to pay." But when situations are reverse and we find ourselves the perpetrator, we seek leniency and mercy and justify our actions.

RECONCILING OFFENSES AND DISAGREEMENTS.

A program called <u>Beyond Scared Straight</u> that features inmates of violent crimes running a program to adjust the course of wayward youth from entering the penal system reminded me of this commandment. The program is extreme but the methods are effective. And so it goes for every revolution. Translated to enterprise, it's the decision to take responsibility for our actions. Resolution may not repair or undo the deed but it offers some dignity back to humanity; to the victims and for the violators. This is from the mild on up to the extreme cases of offense.

Remember human emotions can erupt into infernos kindled by small sparks. And all too often it's an accumulation of these "sparks" that consumes an individual or group to an outbreak of the most shameful displays of insensitivity and heartlessness you will ever want to see. To think by saying, "I'm sorry" as the one size that fits all resolution is repulsive and makes those words common. Actually, saying "I'm sorry" is the same as saying, I'm sorrowful. These feelings do little for the other injured party involved. We can't reconcile offenses unless there are actions to take responsibility, restore, and reconcile ourselves to one another.

Community service is restitution service. It is more tangible and weighty toward the benefit of the enterprising community for everyone to be more "careful" and less sorrowful. This is not to minimize sympathy, it does have its place but to couple it with responsibility to resolve any trespass caused knowingly or unknowingly by anyone within your enterprise.

DEALING WITH WHAT'S DEALT

Don't let your enterprise be ran with absolutely "no hands on" whatsoever. Even the one-minute manager would appreciate this. Furthermore, keep short accounts. Nip things in the bud before it becomes a "bloom of doom." Also be swift in the areas of violation. If you spare the "rule" you'll spoil the brood. Every enterprise should be responsive in accordance with their organizational assets; which is relational capital. Your enterprise's economy will run smooth on a healthy balance of perpetual reward and swift punishments. Some things in business can be open for ruling out but this issue is not one of them.

Resolving conflict takes firmness, guts and tact. It involves a balance of justice and mercy to manage seemingly irreconcilable situations. And with the controversial, uncompromising, no nonsense approach to bring the wood sort to speak, you should know the risks last resorts and its liabilities. This is a responsibility of accountability for everyone to uphold a code of conduct for the betterment not to the detriment of an enterprise and its stakeholders. This is an adjustment one should never be sorry for.

THE COMMANDMENT OF NEWNESS

Change is not a Component, it's a Constant. One side comes like an assault, the other like an aid. The goal is to not let the agency of change become a stranger. (**Scripture:** *"Count it all joy the various trials...they come to perfect...so that you will not lack."***James 1:2***)* Change is the escort of our everyday experiences; whether good or bad, significant or remotely plain. It's no respecter of persons, place or thing. It is emotionless like an angel who is dispatched with orders from heaven. It doesn't care either way decisions are made, it comes with no inside knowledge as to what to expect after it comes.

"Change Has Two Faces:
One is Adversarial, the Other an Ally."

CHANGE ARRIVES, WHETHER YOU'RE READY OR NOT.

Under these circumstances, your best bet is to not fight change or thwart its course. However, we can be student's and enlist ourselves as change agents. Change doesn't have to be a stranger if we embraced it like a frequent traveler that you welcome as a guest. And once its affects has transformed our settings and outlook, we will find its visits don't change our "outward" backdrop as much as it changes our "inner" being upon the way we perceive the world around us.

The environment of all business enterprise go through a unique process of transformation. Some of these changes are predictable as with certain elements of nature; like the planting of trees or the migrating of birds. Certain patterns leave clues to the processes and stages of change; (*the phrase success leaves clues come to mind*). These patterns can provide formulas that can teach one how to apply certain principles toward good business practices involving change.

THE COMMANDMENT OF NURTURING

Discouragement is Fatigue of Motivation. It's like the subtle pain that sets in the muscles and joints having just accomplished great feats. It is a common occurrence. The knowledgeable have discovered that just as an athlete feeds his muscles within 30 minutes after a workout, so should an exhausted spirit be "nourished" with encouragement - whether in victory or defeat -at the beginning and towards the end.

"Encouragement Is The Best Nourishment."

ENCOURAGEMENT IS PROFOUND.

For instance, relationally friends can surround you but a timely word from strangers can lift one's spirit and sustain them through the day -words like HAVE A GOOD DAY! It also doesn't require much time or effort to give a pep talk, a pat on the back or just listening *through* a conversation.

ENCOURAGEMENT IS THE ART OF GROOMING.

Discouragement compared to ticks and lice sets in on us to demoralize through subtlety. And before you know it, we all start itching and scratching from the same causes. Encouragement's potential moves with compassion from one person who has experienced discomfort to another in discouragement. They may have a bedside manner to better care for others because of an association with a similar experience. In other words, they know where to scratch where it itches. Yes, you can encourage yourself and lift yourself up but there are some places that are out of your reach . However, you may find yourself: in over your head, in too deep, in the storms of adversity. This is the time when "others" can be as brothers within an enterprise. The term "I got your back" applies to maintaining a setting that keeps morale high and discouragement low.

LISTENING FOR UNDERSTANDING

There is the ability to hear and the skill of understanding. The apparatus of the ear functions as a capturing funnel for hearing sounds. But the skill of understanding requires listening with full attendance of presence. It's the capacity to listen with your whole heart, mind and body.

LISTENING IS A GIFT WE GIVE OTHERS

Here is a simple acronym to use when encouraging others within your enterprise: Give an **E.A.R**

1. Show **EMPATHY**

   -be present with *someone not present in someone's emotion*

2. Give **ACKNOWLEDGEMENT**

   -reciprocate only what they *communicate as feedback*

3. Wait to **RESPOND**

   -stay neutral, don't rescue or fix them for your sake.

Remember nurturing within an enterprise isn't stroking one's ego, catering to emotion or paternalism. Encouragement is the supply of what's essential in the development of esteeming and restoring the highest value of dignity to those who may fall prey to the self-punishment of shame and guilt.

PRACTICE: Slow to Speak, Quick to Listen!

THE COMMANDMENT OF TRANSLATION

Tools Amplify Inherent Abilities. One hallmark of being ingenious is to translate difficult, complex things into simple terms. The expertise however will be evident when you can remove any evidence of condescension to the learned and patronizing to the uninformed. The ultimate goal is to involve others by providing space. It is translating listeners into learners; doubters into debaters. Insecurity and self-serving natures will cause disruption in translation. The focus must be on your audience and not your eloquence; their need to know not one's need to show.

"Show and Tell then Shut Up"

FACTS TELL BUT STORIES SELL

The humbled mind still knows its place amongst the simple. And true appreciation goes to that person who captured us through simplifying weighty things. Your enterprise will do well with a storyteller of its progress. Most enterprises carry organization assets acquired over time. These assets are portfolios of plans, developments, systems and processes that provide history from then to now. No doubt they serve a purpose in the field of legalese and compliance but to the simple such things are dry, exhausting and too overwhelming. Fact of the matter, the masses follow the highlights - in attention grabbing -short bursts.

COMPETING WITH A SHORT ATTENTION

Keeping it short is sweet. Brevity is not only for the simple but for the elite, the go-getter and the go giver. Making it plain can be a pain for the wordy-windbag. The best approach to simplifying things is shutting out distractions; distractions in thinking and distraction in word usage. The second step is cutting to the chase. In other words, get to the point. Points are prods that trigger painful or pleasurable emotions through what you're communicating. Most times one word blurbs, catch phrases, slogans, quips and quotes will do the trick of summing up a thing.

Mean what you say. Say what your mean,

#8 *You Should Finish*
THE COMMANDMENT OF COMPLETION

Anything Worth Doing Should Be Done Well. Well implies that it was done correctly. Everything started should finish somewhere and at sometime. The only thing that last s forever is eternity. And we're not there because we're fixed in time. The goal is to get one's to do's, to done, by today or at sometime. There is an attitude that says "Anything worth doing should be done right." Maybe your finding yourself "finished" before the project is; (that is your deadline finishing you off before your finish it). Let's look a little more into working on making finishing touches to the starts in your enterprise.

"A Start is a Trial on Everything that has been Prepared."

Ever wonder why we witness massive "recalls" of consumer products from the market place. Products ranging from the defective baby car seat to the automobiles with a faulty brake system somehow manage to slip through the tests. These recalls are a direct result of neglect in the monitoring and controlling.

This principle applies to life also. You may find areas of your life that are missing important pieces like specialized knowledge about a skill set you possess. Or having defective parts of a certain practice of planning that produces short-run-results. These are crooked roads paved with good intentions. They are incomplete, arrested-developments stalled-out on the roadside as memorials of good initiative but bad judgment. It is the failure of finishing and finishing strong.

It is not enough to start out well. We must see it through to its end; if we want to capture the prize. It is the prize of wearing the crown of credibility. It is the success of sustainability. This prize is not allusive. On the contrary, it is quite attainable when practical methods and common practices are in place.

IT'S NOT ABOUT THE RUN; IT'S ALL ABOUT THE RACE.

In order for your enterprise to make a good show for itself, it will need to make a *good go* of things. Here is the list to prequalify.

1. *Count the Cost*

   - Every dollar goes as a registration fee to <u>Enter the Race</u>

2. *Commit to Task*

   - Every effort goes as human equity to <u>Run the Race</u>

3. *Change when Needed*

   - Every adjustment goes as to <u>Study the Race</u>

4. *Complete the Cycle*

   - Every start goes to <u>Finish the Race</u>

Before starting, count the cost of finishing every venture. Then decide to **S.T.I.C**: Stay Till Its Complete.

THE COMMANDMENT OF INTEREST

Invest In The Field, Then Build The Dream. Your Time, Talent, Treasures and Tools are your only stocks for trade. And sweat may be the only return on your investment during the initial start up stages. Everyone possesses measures of something. These benefits are creatively given to us all. These commodities can grow through good investment vehicles. The worst scenario is to not invest at all. This is not becoming involved in adding interest toward oneself or others at all.

"The Resource of an Outgoing Source Brings Income+Interest."

BEGIN TO DEVELOP AN EYE FOR VALUE.

Develop a redemptive eye that sees commodity in the oddity. The copy company Kinko's brand is the founder's nickname, given for his "kinky" curly hair. And the rest is a profitable history. These are those diamonds in the rough, or pearls of great price stories. It's been said that one should cultivate his true gift but also nurture his talents. Talents die with us and are taken to the grave but gifts keep on giving interest long after we retire. The emphasis here is to make personal investments your first priority. Just the simple investment of a college education more than doubles your personal earning worth. And a nest egg doesn't do you any good if you don't allow an investment vehicle to sit on it (*softly as to not crush*) and add warm giving compounded interest until it hatches.

DON'T DESPISE SMALL BEGINNINGS

Size does matter. And SMALL is the new big! Small is manageable. Small is measureable. Small is magical. Remember profitability is measured by percentages. The law of averages will give you a percentage after your conversion rates kick in from your frequency of efforts. There is also the diminishing effect of small. These are leaks that compound over time if not accounted for.

ADVICE: Stay out of the heap of "failures" that refused to invest wisely and remember getting big is a natural result of going slow from starting small.

#10 *You Should Reward*
THE COMMANDMENT OF CELEBRATION

Depravity is a sin; as is Overindulgence. Reward comes in many forms other than the tangible materialist ones; money, vacations, plaques and gold watches. Intangible things like praise, honor, recognition and favor come with different price tags. Whether tangible or not, they are rewards that are intended to be claimed and released to those who have deserved them. Most of our lives are conducted under the pretense, if we do what is required, we will be rewarded. And if we make sound investments we can expect good returns.

"Hope Deferred Makes The Heart Sick."

STAKING CLAIMS AND RELEASING REWARDS

America has its share of debt. And a lot will be required of us to pay it down. But it also has benefits and rewards that go unclaimed which is just as important as the debt issue. There are private estates that are unclaimed. Inheritances trapped in probate. Unknown fortunes are awarded to the state. This is a reflection of what happens to an enterprise who forgets their history and are robbed of their environmental assets On the other hand, there is injustice where claims are *not* released and are held hostage by the same legal actions that gives us our freedoms; manipulated as vices to withhold what is due to those rightfully deserving.

RENDER WHAT IS DUE

No doubt injustice does exist and ignorance of our inheritance and true worth persist but it shouldn't prevail over rendering respect of what is deserved. Render what is due to every person in honor, in customs and especially in wages. This is how we balance the deficit of our personal and extended community's economic values. More than profits, portfolios and projections is the national treasures of personal sacrifice and the commitment of human equity. These first, not last, are to be celebrated.

FINAL INCLUSIONS

The law of the letter kills but the spirit of it makes alive ...

Rules weren't made to be broken. They were made to build, preserve and provide direction to suit one's vision, goals and dreams. Whatever your enterprise, industry or practice, never sacrifice the vision or your mission to preserve your precious rules. Instead, <u>Reform</u> them as in tailoring to facilitate the size of your growth. <u>Review</u> them to accommodate the changing needs of your marketplace. And Lastly, <u>Revisit</u> them for reflection. With any endeavor worth enterprising there comes long before the rules, roles and regulations were written, there were relationships. And these relationships are the real systems, involving real people that really keep things reigned in.

www.ingramcontent.com/pod-product-compliance
Lightning Source LLC
Chambersburg PA
CBHW030012190526
45157CB00015B/2492